A Parent's Guide to Home and School SUCCESS

THIRD GRADE

Written by
Glenda Frasier

Illustrations by
Marilee Harrald-Pilz

Cover Photo by Bruce Ayres / Stone. Copyright © Stone.

Photo Credits: © 1997 Comstock, Inc.: 3, 8, 11, 21, 33, 35, 36, 38, 41

Copyright © 1997
This version copyright © 2000 Brighter Vision Publications.
All rights reserved. Except for the inclusion of brief quotations in a review, no part of this book may be reproduced or utilized in any form or by any means, electronic or mechanical, including photocopying, recording, or by any information storage and retrieval system, without written permission from the publisher.

BV15033 Home and School Successs: Third Grade
Published by Brighter Vision Publications, 225 Duncan Mill Road, Don Mills, Ontario, Canada M3B 3K9
TM is a trademark of Brighter Vision Publications.
Printed in the U.S.A.

Table of Contents

Introduction

The Thrilling Third Grader 1
The Keys to Using This Book 2

Academic Skills

Reading 3–7
Language Arts 8–15
Math 16–20
Science 21–24
Social Studies 25–28
Art 29–30
Music 31–32
Physical Education 33–34

Social Skills

Respect 35–36
Responsibilty 37
Classroom Interactions 38
Problem Solving 39

Home and School Cooperation

Communication 40–41
Creating Cooperative
Conferences 42
Volunteering 43
Homework 44

Rewards

Bookmark Rewards 45–46

The Thrilling Third Grader!

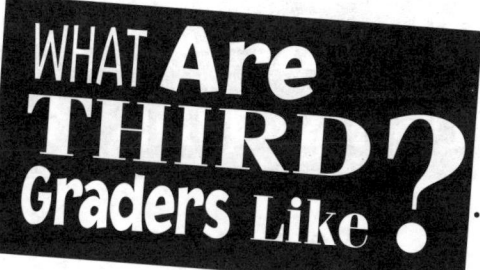

Parents wear many hats every day. Each one is equally important, but sometimes parents are nervous about wearing the hat of "teacher" for their child. The truth is that all day every day the invisible "teacher hat" is perched on your head, perhaps even on top of another hat you may be wearing at the moment! The joy of parenting comes with making the most of every opportunity to be your child's "teacher."

Parents can be nervous about performing the role of teacher because they are not sure what expectations or goals are realistic for their child at each level. This book is aimed at helping you understand, appreciate, and accentuate the learning that your child is ready to experience.

You were and still are your child's first and most important teacher. By becoming familiar with the skills a third grader needs, you can be more efficient and effective as you continue in that role.

What Are Third Graders Like?

* They are **honest** both in compliments and complaints. They express opinions without hesitation.

* They are **imaginative**. Give them a box of odds 'n' ends and watch the creations develop.

* They are **remarkable**. Their capacity to live and learn and love is bottomless.

* They are **determined**. Involve them in a project or event and watch the commitment emerge!

* They are **gracious** with others and seek many friendships with people of all ages.

* They are **risk takers**. They like to be the leaders and investigate new horizons.

* They are **anxious** to be the best they can be and need constant encouragement.

* They are **discoverers**. Problem solving becomes an adventure to be conquered.

* They are **exuberant**. Their curiosity propels them into learning with vitality.

* They are **ready** to learn and grow with your direction and the ideas in this book.

BV15033 Home and School Success: Third Grade • Brighter Vision Publications • 1

The Keys to Using This Book

 Be a Learner
Be ready to tell your child that you don't know something. A question from your child indicates interest in the topic, but you don't need to feel embarrassed if you don't know the answer. The important step is to help them look for an answer.

 Teach to the Moment
Remember that the best time to teach anything is the moment your child has expressed curiosity about it. If your child asks a question about the phases of the moon, try to provide information, look it up with him or her in a science book or encyclopedia, and watch the sky. If you have access to the Internet or a computer with a multimedia reference tool, use that to gain instant facts to share.

 Teach Academic Skills
The first section of this book provides a guide for you full of activities that center around the topics third graders study in school. Use it to help your child better understand a topic that is being taught and to enhance what your child is learning at school. Use it as background information to provide ideas for you to use when interacting with your child.

 Teach Social Skills
The next section centers around social skills. Even the most intelligent child will be less successful in school without good personal skills. These interpersonal skills are critical for positive relationships to develop and for your child to feel worthwhile. Use this section to provide an approach to a problem or an opening to discuss a topic. With prior discussion about these vital skills, your child will have strategies to deal with concerns when they appear.

 Promote Home and School Cooperation
The next section of this book gives you practical ideas for how to navigate home and school interaction on a daily basis. There are suggestions for organizing, communicating with the educational community, conferencing with teachers, and getting involved at school.

 Give Praise
Included in the book are reward items. Use these to show your child that you are proud of his or her efforts. Children respond to positive reinforcement. Teachers know that the more specific the praise, the better. "Good job!" is great to hear, but more repeat performances come from phrases such as "You wrote your story so neatly that it is easy for me to read. That shows me you are proud of it, too!"

Reading Skills Third Graders Need

PHONICS, WORD ANALYSIS, AND VOCABULARY

* Recognize and use consonant blends at the beginning of words (Ex: *br-, pl-, scr-, st-*)
* Recognize and use consonant blends at the end of words (Ex: *-nt, -ld*)
* Recognize and use consonant digraphs [two letters that make one sound] at the beginning and end of words (Ex: *th, ch, sh*)
* Recognize and use long and short vowels in words
* Recognize that two vowels together may make a special sound of their own (Ex: *oy* in *boy*; *ou* in *pout*; *au* in *haul*; *ew* in *new*)
* Recognize and use endings on words, such as *-ed, -s, -es, -ing, -er, -est*
* Understand that words are made of parts, or beats, called syllables and that each syllable has at least one vowel (Ex: *child,* one syllable; *par ent,* two syllables)
* Identify contractions and the words they are made of (Ex: *can't–can not, I'm–I am*)
* Understand possessives, such as *Susie's bicycle* or *the boys' bats*
* Recognize rhyming words
* Recognize spelling patterns in words, such as *coat, poach, throat*
* Recognize compound words
* Understand synonyms [words that mean about the same] (Ex: *grin* and *smile*)
* Understand antonyms [words that mean the opposite] (Ex: *happy* and *sad*)
* Understand homophones [words that sound alike but have different meanings and spellings] (Ex: *pear* and *pair*)
* Understand that some words that look alike may have different meanings, such as *bank* (land along a water's edge) and *bank* (a place where money is kept)

COMPREHENSION

* Understand that a paragraph has a main idea and supporting details
* Recall details from text
* Predict what will happen next
* Sequence the events in the story
* Summarize the main points in a story
* Develop an ability to explain cause and effect
* Draw logical conclusions from their reading
* Know the difference between fact and opinion
* Know the difference between fiction and nonfiction
* Tell the meaning of common expressions
* Read and follow directions
* Use drawings, maps, and charts that accompany the text to help understand it
* Draw pictures or diagrams to explain the text

BV15033 Home and School Success: Third Grade • Brighter Vision Publications • 3

VENTURING THROUGH VOWEL LAND!

Vowels are *a, e, i, o, u* and sometimes *y*. Vowels make a variety of sounds in words.

If you pretend that a word is like a jelly sandwich, the consonants are the bread and the vowels are the jelly. The consonants make the framework of the word, and the vowels give the word a special "flavor" or uniqueness that lets us discriminate that word from other words.

For example, look at these frames: a) s__d b) m__n. The first word could be sad, sod, said, seed, or sued. The second word could be man, men, main, mean, or moon. We don't know for sure until we add the vowels.

Third graders need to advance beyond short and long vowels and gain competency recognizing other vowel sounds, such as digraphs (sch*oo*l, b*oo*k, y*aw*n) diphthongs (*ou*t, j*oy*, n*ew*) r-controlled vowels (h*er*, st*are*, w*or*d), and the schwa sound (*a*bout, th*e*, *o*ther).

Because vowels can make so many different sounds, some children have difficulty with them. Help your child if you see specific vowel sounds that are problematic.

A great way to practice vowels with your child is to point out tricky combinations as you read together. When the word "terror" appears, you can mention the "r-controlled" vowels that are found in that word. Whenever "Bossy R" follows a vowel, it changes the sound the vowel makes. The repetition your child sees and hears in literature will help cement the phonics rules that are taught at school.

VOWEL TIC-TAC-TOE

Each player selects a vowel sound to practice, for example *ou* and *ea*. (You may want to check with your child's teacher on specific sounds to work with.) The game is played just like tic-tac-toe except players write words with their corresponding vowel sound, rather than X's or O's.

The winner in this game is the *ou* player who wrote three *ou* words in a row.

VOWEL BOWLING

For this activity you need a set of plastic bowling pins and a ball. (These are available at discount stores in the toy department or sometimes at yard sales.) Use a permanent marker to write vowel letters or combinations on each pin. Set them up and join your child in a game of bowling. For every pin knocked down, the player must give a word with that vowel sound in it. For every word that is correct, a point is awarded. The winner is the bowler with the most points at the end of the ten rolls.

CONTRACTIONS

* As you read with your child, point out contractions in the stories. Reread the sentence substituting the two words for the contraction. Ask how the sentences are different. Is one way better than the other? Do the sentences mean the same thing?

* Use a red marker to circle contractions you find in the newspaper.

Contractions are shortened words that are made by combining words, leaving out one or more letters, and putting an apostrophe in their place.
Example: is + not = isn't

* Write contractions like these on a piece of paper. Have your child identify the two words that make up each contraction.

he'll	wasn't	I've	she'll
wouldn't	you've	it's	didn't
could've	that's	don't	we're
who's	won't	they're	I'd
needn't	I'm	you'd	can't

ANTONYMS

A mastery of antonyms helps your child read and write better. It increases the listening and speaking vocabulary which in turn increases comprehension. To practice antonyms try these games:

Antonym Checkers—Using a regular checkerboard, either write one word on each square or write the word on self-sticking notes and lay them on the squares.

The object of the game is to pronounce the word and give an "opposite" every time your checker lands on that square.

Antonym Hide and Seek—Write each of the antonyms listed below on separate cards. Hide half of each antonym pair in a specified area, like the living room or the backyard. Give your child the other set of cards. The object is for your child to find the hidden words and match the opposites.

Antonyms are words that mean the opposite.
Example: stop-go

day-night	black-white	sad-happy	sun-moon
catch-throw	clean-dirty	open-shut	smile-frown
up-down	silly-serious	on-off	noisy-quiet
pull-push	straight-crooked	good-bad	first-last
part-whole	shiny-dull	front-back	never-always
walk-run	broken-repaired	sit-stand	win-lose
play-work	light-heavy	hard-soft	sink-float

SEARCH!

Help your child get the most out of every reading activity. No matter what kind of text needs to be read the SEARCH method will help your child get the meaning! It gets the reader's mind set on what will be read.

Teach your child to do these steps:

SCAN—Look over the information from start to finish. Take a look at the pictures and predict what is going to happen.

EXAMINE—Read the bold print, questions along the side, and paragraph or chapter headings. Think about the way the book or article is put together.

ASK—Ask questions about what you saw. How does it fit together? Why did the author choose that title? How do the pictures fit with the story? Ask yourself the questions or ask a reading partner. Jot them down if you like.

READ—Now you are ready to read the text word for word. Watch punctuation and sentence structure.

CHECK—Check yourself on your reading. See if you can answer the questions you asked in the beginning. Did you understand what you read? Draw a picture of what you read, make a chart about the article, or write a few sentences about the story.

HELP—Get help if you didn't understand what you read. Ask an adult, look up the topic in another book or encyclopedia, or talk about it with a friend.

Once you understand, **celebrate** your learning.

Make several copies of this bookmark for your child to use while reading.

Wonderful Books for Third Graders to Explore

These books may be found at your school or public library. They would make perfect gifts for any occasion. Check your local bookstore. You will enjoy these, too!

Picture Books

Annie and the Old One by Miska Miles (Little, Brown, 1971)

Cloudy with a Chance of Meatballs by Judith Barrett (Macmillan, 1982)

Family Pictures/Cuadros de familia by Carmen Lomas Garza (Children's Book Press, 1990)

Grandfather Tang's Story by Ann Tompert (Crown, 1990)

Hershel and the Hanukkah Goblins by Eric A. Kimmel (Holiday, 1989)

The Great Kapok Tree by Lynne Cherry (Harcourt Brace Jovanovich, 1990)

Miss Rumphius by Barbara Cooney (Viking, 1982)

Chapter Books

Freckle Juice by Judy Blume (Macmillan, 1971)

How to Eat Fried Worms by Thomas Rockwell (Watts, 1973)

Mr. Popper's Penguins by Richard & Florence Atwater (Little, Brown, 1938)

Sarah, Plain and Tall by Patricia MacLachlan (Harper & Row, 1985)

Sideways Stories From Wayside School by Louis Sachar (Random House, 1990)

The Twenty-One Balloons by William Pene du Bois (Viking, 1947)

...and thousands more!

Folklore

Her Stories: African American Folktales, Fairy Tales, and True Tales by Virginia Hamilton (Scholastic, 1995)

The Adventures of Robin Hood by Marcia Williams (Candlewick, 1995)

The Stinky Cheese Man and Other Fairly Stupid Tales by Jon Scieszka (Viking, 1992)

Poetry

Night on Neighborhood Street by Eloise Greenfield (Dial, 1991)

Something Big Has Been Here by Jack Prelutsky (Greenwillow, 1990)

Where the Sidewalk Ends by Shel Silverstein (Harper & Row, 1974)

These authors have written many books that Third Graders will enjoy:

Picture Books

Harry Allard	Paul Goble
Mitsumasa Anno	William Steig
Molly Bang	Chris Van Allsburg
Jan Brett	Judith Viorst
Carol Carrick	Jane Yolen
Joanna Cole	

Informational Books

Aliki
George Ancona
Franklyn Branley
Jean Fritz
Gail Gibbons
Jill Krementz
Ellen Levine
Mike Venezia
Kate Waters

Chapter Books

Beverly Cleary
Roald Dahl
Mary Pope Osborne
Barbara Park
Daniel M. Pinkwater
Dick King-Smith
Donald Sobol

Language Arts Skills Third Graders Need

WRITING

* Understand what makes a complete sentence
* Understand that a paragraph is made of a main idea sentence and supporting sentences
* Create stories with a beginning, middle, and end
* Use descriptive words to create a picture for the reader
* Include details about setting, theme, plot, and characters in the writing
* Include who, what, where, when, why, and how in a composition
* Write a report on a nonfiction topic
* Write a friendly letter
* Address an envelope
* Create poetry
* Follow a step-by-step process for writing
* Understand that each piece of writing may have a specific audience
* Edit writing that is for others to read
* Write legibly
* Capitalize words correctly
* Use punctuation correctly
* See themselves as writers
* Enjoy sharing their writing with others in a variety of ways

SPELLING

* Spell basic sight words
* Understand that the same sound may have a variety of spellings
* Apply basic spelling rules
* Follow a step-by-step process to learn to spell new words
* Use phonics and spelling skills to locate words in a dictionary or spell checker

GRAMMAR

* Recognize that nouns are names of people, places, and things
* Recognize that proper nouns are the names of special people, places, or things and need to be capitalized
* Recognize action words as verbs
* Recognize adjectives as words that describe
* Understand that a sentence has a subject and a predicate

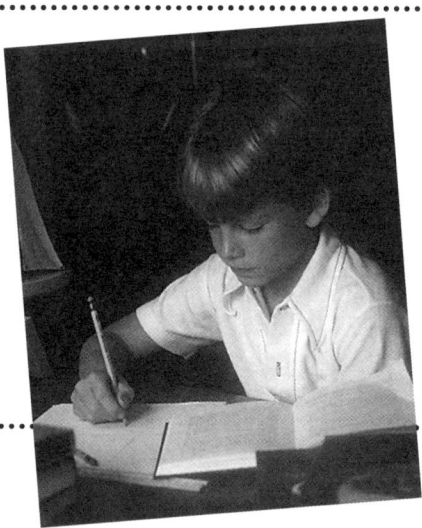

PENMANSHIP

* Write neatly using manuscript alphabet (printing)
* Form letters correctly
* Practice cursive writing

THE WRITING PROCESS

Many teachers show students a five-step process for writing. While the writing process may vary, these are the primary steps to follow.

Prewriting
* Brainstorm ideas
* Ask questions
* Research the topic
* Talk about it with others
* Share ideas
* Make a list of words you may need
* Jot down notes
* Draw a picture
* Make a mind web to categorize the ideas

Draft writing
* Focus on the ideas you want to include
* Write phrases, sentences, and paragraphs
* Stress content and ideas not structure at this point

Talk and Share
* Read it to a partner or teacher
* Discuss changes
* Look for new ways to write something
* Check for audience understanding
* Confer with others

Edit
* Revise sentences
* Elaborate on details
* Enhance words you chose
* Connect the ideas
* Proofread for spelling, structure, grammar, punctuation, and capital letters

Publish
* Rewrite using the revised draft
* Create a final draft
* Share it with a group or the class
* Make a book
* Display it on a bulletin board
* Tape record or videotape it

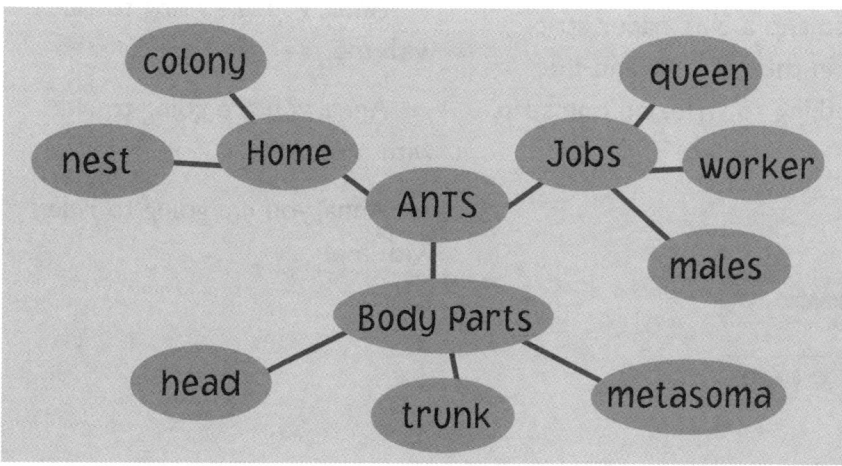

A mind web gives the learner a visual way to think about the topic. It can be simple or very elaborate, but its purpose is to give structure to the writing.

USING COMPLETE SENTENCES

Before third graders can write complete sentences, they must be able to speak in complete sentences. Insist that your child use complete sentences in discussions and speak to them in complete sentences. There will certainly be times in family conversation when complete sentences or answers are not feasible. Whenever possible, however, model correct language because that is the best way to teach it. Do not criticize your child's language, just repeat it correctly and ask him or her to say it again.

The next step is to recognize sentence fragments and complete sentences. Write or say some partial sentences and see if your child can identify the error. If this is difficult, draw a diagram and let your child fill in the parts. Third graders can usually label the subject (whom or what the sentence is about), predicate (what the subject is doing), and adjectives (words that describe).

Example: Silly frogs eat peanut butter.

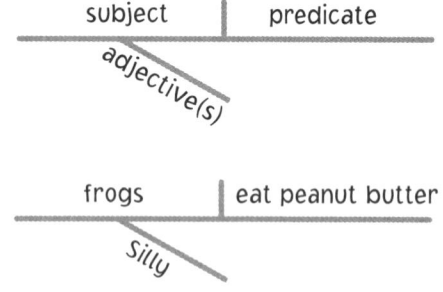

✻ For a hands-on activity, cut out a red and a blue paper strip. Write the subject of the sentence on the red one, and the predicate on the blue. If there is nothing to write on one strip, then the sentence is not complete.

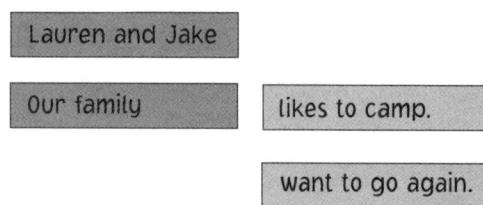

TYPES OF SENTENCES

Third graders are learning that there are different types of sentences.

✻ Telling sentence (statement)

✻ Asking sentence (question)

✻ Exciting sentence (exclamation)

As you ride in the car or wait in line at the grocery store, tell your child a sentence. Ask what kind of sentence it is and what punctuation should go at the end.

✻ Telling sentence—period

✻ Asking sentence—question mark

✻ Exciting sentence—exclamation point

While reading with your child, point out the variety of sentences that are found in the story. Ask your child to describe what kind of sentence each one is. Point out the punctuation that is used.

Use sentences like these to demonstrate the difference punctuation makes:

Anna, you are going to ride with me.

Anna, you are going to ride with me?

Anna, you *are* going to ride with me!

EDITING STRATEGIES

Third graders understand that writing has different purposes and different audiences. Sometimes a writer is composing just for himself. That is often a rough draft or just notes. Sometimes a writer clearly wants others to read the work. In that case, errors should be minimal. To achieve this higher level of writing, writers edit their work to make corrections, improve the wording, and make the writing ready to be published. This is a final draft.

Editing is a long procedure if done carefully. It does not need to be done for every single piece of writing. When your child has an assignment to be turned in for a grade, that is an important piece of writing which will be read by others. Thus editing becomes a part of the assignment.

Adults must be patient enough to include editing as a vital step in the writing process. To save you and your child tears, make sure you don't schedule writing, editing, and rewriting a long assignment all in the same night.

It helps speed the process if the learner has a formula to follow to add consistency and accuracy. Copy the chart on the right and place it at your child's work space or enlarge it and make a wall poster! Keep this strategy handy for every writing activity until it becomes a habit for your child to use with any final draft.

SCOPE IT!
S: Check your sentences.
C: Check the capital letters.
O: Check the order.
P: Check the punctuation.
E: EXCELLENT EDITING!

S is for sentence structure.
* Is every sentence complete?
* Do the sentences make sense?
* Is there a main idea sentence?
* Does each sentence add new information?

C is for capital letters.
* Does every sentence start with a capital letter?
* Do proper nouns (the names of special people, places or things) begin with a capital letter?

O is for order and organization.
* Is there a beginning, middle, and end to the writing?
* Does the order make sense?

P is for punctuation.
* Does every sentence end with the proper punctuation: period, question mark, or exclamation point?
* Are there quotation marks around the exact words someone says?
* Are commas and apostrophes used correctly?

E is for EXCELLENT!

Great job of editing your work! Celebrate and share your work with EVERYONE!!!

SPEAKING UP!

Many times children are expected to share their writing or other work aloud. Speaking to a group or the entire class is an important, and often scary, facet of the language arts curriculum. If your child is afraid to speak up in class, it helps to talk about it. During the conversation, discuss what is the cause of the fear.

If your child is extremely shy, suggest picturing a classroom event in which your child gives a successful report or speaks up successfully in class. Visualization is a technique used by many star athletes that helps them reach their goals.

If other children have laughed at your child, suggest that these students may think laughing at others helps make the teasers braver. Encourage your child to react with humor instead of becoming shy or angry.

If your child thinks he or she is not smart enough to speak up, make a list of all the areas where your child has truly excelled. Express pride in these accomplishments.

If your child is afraid of making a mistake, try these ideas:

* Request that the teacher repeat the question.

* Be sure to be well prepared. Ask yourself questions that the teacher might ask the next day about the material you read.

If your child hates being stared at, teach "deflection" strategies:

* Choose one friend to speak to as you give a report.

* Pick out one face in the back to address.

* Look at the back wall of the room or scan the room with your eyes without really focusing on any one person.

If your child thinks no one is interested in what he or she might say, model interest at home and show that you care about what is said. For example, during a conversation with your child, make sure you are truly focused on your child, not the television or the newspaper.

If your child is still concerned, organize a practice session at home during which you and your child act out

speaking situations. Tell your child that fear can be conquered in this case by even "pretending" that speaking is comfortable. Have your child name a celebrity he or she admires and pretend to be that person giving the talk. Your child can become confident and successful at speaking up even if it is "acting."

What if your child talks too much?

* Model good conversation techniques.

* Point out that good conversation requires taking turns.

* Remind your child to respond to what is said.

* Suggest that your child include questions for the listener.

* Describe conversation as a partnership among two or more people.

* Let your child witness and participate in effective adult conversation.

SPELLING

Develop a step-by-step procedure for learning to spell a word. Help your child follow that pattern consistently. Here is a suggested routine. Copy this and place it on the refrigerator right next to the spelling list your child brings home from school.

I can learn to spell any word!
1. I look at the word.
2. I say the word.
3. I write the word.
4. I check the word.
5. I spell the word aloud.
6. I use the word in a sentence.
7. I watch for the word in a book or newspaper.
8. I use the word in a story I am writing.

MY OWN DICTIONARY

Help your child start a dictionary of words that are personal spelling demons. Use a notebook or note pad, or staple 13 sheets of paper together. Label each page with a letter of the alphabet.

As you review schoolwork, assist with homework, or read a story your child wrote, encourage him or her to jot down any misspelled words.

When any of those words are required again in a piece of writing, the dictionary is there to refer to for the correct spelling. It is quicker than using a large dictionary. Research shows that writers often repeat specific words and this will help your child be assured of accuracy.

Include a short phrase for the meaning of words like *their*, *there*, and *they're*. Homophones are difficult for third graders to spell correctly.

Be sure your child pronounces words correctly. If you hear "are" when the word should be "our," repeat the sentence and model the correct pronunciation.

Reward your child's progress in spelling with one of the bookmarks in this book or a special treat of your choice.

PENMANSHIP

Learning and practicing cursive handwriting is an important activity in third grade. There are two major styles of cursive handwriting —regular and contempory. Both are included in this book for your reference. Check with your child's teacher to see which style your school uses.

REGULAR CURSIVE

Aa   Bb   Cc   Dd

Ee   Ff   Gg   Hh

Ii   Jj   Kk   Ll

Mm   Nn   Oo   Pp

Qq   Rr   Ss   Tt

Uu   Vv   Ww   Xx

Yy   Zz

CONTEMPORARY CURSIVE

Aa Bb Cc

Dd Ee Ff Gg

Hh Ii Jj Kk

Ll Mm Nn Oo

Pp Qq Rr Ss

Tt Uu Vv Ww

Xx Yy Zz

Math Skills Third Graders Need

NUMBERS, FACTS, AND COMPUTATION

* Understand place value to one million
* Read and write numbers and number words to one thousand
* Recognize number patterns like these: 2, 3, 5, 6, 8, 9 ... or 6, 12, 18, 24, 30 ...
* Round two-digit numbers to the nearest ten
* Master addition facts (0 + 0 through 9 + 9)
* Master subtraction facts (0 − 0 through 18 − 9)
* Practice multiplication facts
* Practice division facts
* Add and subtract 4-digit numbers
* Add three 2-digit numbers
* Rename or regroup (carrying and borrowing)
* Estimate results and check with a calculator

GEOMETRY, MEASUREMENT, AND FRACTIONS

* Understand symmetry where both halves of a shape or object are the same
* Explore shapes with many sides
* Identify and create geometric patterns
* Estimate distances and amounts
* Compare volume
* Measure length, width, and height to the nearest inch or centimeter
* Use metric and customary measuring instruments
* Recognize fractions: ½, ⅓, ¼, ⅛

MONEY, TIME, AND PROBLEM SOLVING

* Name all coins and bills
* Add and subtract dollars and cents
* Make change and practice counting it back
* Tell time to the nearest minute on both analog and digital clocks
* Understand and use a calendar
* Use different strategies for solving problems—guess and check, find a pattern, draw a picture, act it out, write a math sentence
* Be aware of key words that may indicate which operation to use
* Choose the correct operation needed to solve the problem

NUMERATION

Third graders should be able to read and write numerals to 1000. Here are some fun ways to reinforce numeration.

✸ As you shop at the grocery store, have your child locate items that come in lots of 50, 100, 500, or 1000. Examples: 100 vitamins, 500 cotton swabs. Be sure to note how the amount is written on different products.

✸ Write an amount of money on a slip of paper, such as $142. Let your child browse through catalogs or newspaper inserts and find something to buy that costs exactly that amount of money or a little less. Vary the amount each time you play.

✸ Explore a calendar with your child, pointing out the different number of days in each month. Tell your child to estimate how many days there are in a year. Then add up all the days. Check the answer. Be sure your child says "three hundred sixty-five," not "three hundred *and* sixty-five." (The *and* indicates a decimal point.)

✸ Use play money from a board game you have, such as Monopoly.™ Take turns writing out "bills" to each other listing how much to pay for a chore or activity that was completed that day. Perhaps you owe your child $479 for cleaning the bathrooms and he owes you $392 for making dinner. Each person who receives the bill counts out the amount in play money and has the other person check it. Set the game range between $100 and $1000 to give your child maximum practice.

✸ Use candies or cereal of different colors to practice making numbers. Jelly beans work great for this. First make a workmat like the one below.

Lay down 1 black, 4 reds, and 2 yellows. Your child should write 142 and read *one hundred forty-two*. Take turns giving each other jelly beans and writing and reading the matching numbers. You may want to have your child gather a handful of jelly beans, sort them, and make the matching number. Whenever there are 10 of one color, your child should trade them (regrouping) for one of the next larger color. Use only one green jelly bean to begin with. Once your child is ready, you can add more greens to make greater numbers.

Jelly Bean Numbers

GREEN thousands	BLACK hundreds	RED tens	YELLOW ones

BV15033 Home and School Success: Third Grade • Brighter Vision Publications • 17

MEASUREMENT

To demonstrate the importance of using a standard unit when measuring, have your child walk across the room, heel to toe, counting the steps. Now you do the same. Compare answers. Ask your child, "Why are our numbers different?" A similar activity is to use toothpicks laid end to end to measure the length of a piece of paper. Next lay pencils end to end and measure it. Then use a ruler. Why are all the numbers different? Talk about how measuring things this way would not work. If you ordered a board ten feet long measured by your feet, would the carpenter's feet be the same length as yours?

Show your child a yardstick and a meter stick. (Or substitute a ruler or measuring tape that has both Customary and Metric units.) Compare the different markings. Explain that they are two systems of measurement and it is important to be familiar with both. Inches and feet are known as Customary units and centimeters and meters are Metric units. Compare product labels to find other examples of measurement units (Customary—quarts, pounds, ounces; Metric—liters, kilograms, grams).

Measurement Scavenger Hunt—Do this scavenger hunt to practice measurement.
* Find 5 things that are less than a centimeter long.
* Find 5 things that are more than an inch long.
* Find 5 things that are more than a foot long.
* Find 5 things that are less than a meter long.
* Find something that is about 11 inches high.
* Find something that is about 3 centimeters high.
* Find something that is about 6 centimeters around! Do you need a different measuring tool?

Estimate It!—Estimation is an excellent skill to incorporate with measuring activities. Before your child begins measuring items, ask him or her to "guess" or "predict" the length, height, or the width of a particular item. Then suggest measuring to see how close the estimate was to the real measurement.

Which is more?—Save a liter bottle and a quart jar or measuring cup. (Some measuring cups have both measuring systems on them so you can compare them in one step.) Let your child fill the liter bottle with water and then pour it into the quart jar. Are they the same? Would you rather have one liter of soda or one quart of soda or does it make any difference? Pour the water on a thirsty plant or cook some spaghetti in it when you are finished . . . don't waste it!

Make Measuring Memos—Help your child measure one centimeter on a cardboard strip and cut it out. Use that standard to test measure items he or she finds. Do the same for an inch, foot, yard, and meter. To measure an entire room, your child could cut several yard lengths or meter lengths of cardboard or string and lay them end to end. Discuss why having a ruler or measuring tape is handier than a single individual segment.

FACTS CAN BE FUN!

Practicing math facts is a very important part of learning. It does not have to be boring if you spice up the practice time with some action! Here are some fun ways to practice math facts.

Beach Ball Toss—Purchase an inflatable plastic beach ball. (At the end of the summer you can find them at bargain prices on the clearance tables of discount stores.) Use a marker to write a fact your child needs to practice on each colored section. Check in your child's math text for samples.

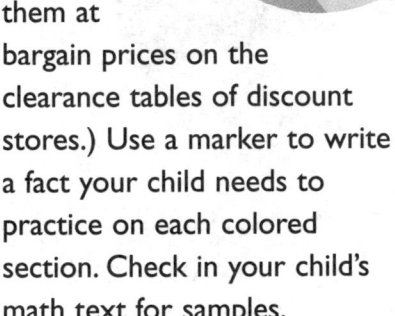

Toss the ball to your child and call out a color. Your child calls out the answer to the fact, tosses the ball back, and calls out a color for you. Once in awhile when it is your turn, call out the wrong answer and see if your child "catches" you in a "miss!"

For variety, put the answer on the ball and have the "catcher" give the problem!

If you use a water-based marker, you can wipe the facts off as they are mastered and add new ones. Water-based markers, however, will rub off on your hands. You may want to purchase several balls and use a permanent marker.

Hopscotch—Draw a hopscotch board on the sidewalk. Write a math fact in each box. Each player tosses a marker and hops down to the box it lands in, saying the answers to the facts as they hop along.

Caution: Have children check their shoes for chalk dust before they enter the house.

> Math facts are the basic addition, subtraction, multiplication, and division problems one needs to know to be able to solve more complex problems. Examples:
> $3 + 2 = 5$ $18 - 9 = 9$
> $6 \times 4 = 24$ $56 \div 8 = 7$

Write and Eat—Write the answer to a math fact on a graham cracker with squeeze-tube icing. Have your child give you the problem and then eat the snack! Be sure your child knows what operation (addition, subtraction, multiplication or division) that is being practiced. For a more nutritional approach, use squirtable cheese on crackers.

Stick Writing—While sitting on the beach, in your yard, or in your driveway, write facts and answers in the sand or dirt with a stick.

Kitchen Writing—Fill a cookie sheet with a thin layer of cornmeal, flour, or salt. Instead of writing math facts on paper, have your child write them in the tray with a finger.

Caution: Salt can corrode metal, so don't leave it on the cookie sheet for long periods of time. Don't reuse any of these substances in cooking after using them this way.

BV15033 Home and School Success: Third Grade • Brighter Vision Publications

STORY PROBLEMS

Teachers will tell you that the most difficult math activity for most students is solving story problems. One reason is that many children do not think through which operations make sense in solving the problem—addition, subtraction, multiplication, or division. A basic concept children should know is that adding or multiplying whole numbers yields equal or greater numbers. Subtracting or dividing yields equal or lesser numbers.

The more practice children have with story problems, the easier they become. When practicing story problems with your child, there are two things to keep in mind:

1. You need to teach strategies to help your child think through and solve the problems.
2. You need to use real-life situations. Use topics that interest your child and personalize them. If you are solving a problem that your child could solve, invite him or her to help you.

Problem-solving Strategies
- Recognize clue words
  Addition—altogether; in all, total
  Subtraction—left, how many more, difference
  Multiplication—altogether; How many in all the sets?
  Division—How many in each set or group?
- Choose an operation (+ − × ÷)
- Find a pattern
- Draw a picture
- Act it out with objects
- Guess and check

Examples:

1. (Your child's name) has in-line skates with 8 wheels on each one. How many wheels are there altogether on the skates? *16 wheels* (8 + 8 = 16 or 8 x 2 = 16; Point out that a problem can often be solved in more than one way.)

2. (Your child's name) has 23 pieces of candy. (A friend of your child) has 17 pieces of candy. How much more candy does (your child) have than (your child's friend)? *6 pieces more* (23 − 17 = 6)

3. Every child in the first row in the third grade classroom at (your child's school) has 4 yellow pencils. There are 6 children in the first row. If they put all their pencils together in one pencil box, how many pencils would there be? *24 pencils* (4 + 4 + 4 + 4 + 4 + 4 = 24 or 4 x 6 = 24)

4. At lunch, (your child's name) wants to share his/her bag of marshmallows with (friend) and (friend). There are 18 marshmallows in the bag. How many will each child get?
6 marshmallows (18 ÷ 3 = 6)

Remember, pictures often get the message across better than words. Have your child draw a picture of what the problem is describing and what it is asking. It can be just a quick sketch that will add meaning to help determine which operation to use.

Science and Health Skills Third Graders Need

LIFE SCIENCE, EARTH SCIENCE, AND PHYSICAL SCIENCE

* Predict
* Observe
* Classify and measure
* Collect and organize data
* Draw conclusions
* Understand seeds and the process of germination
* Understand the difference between living and non-living
* Understand the food chain
* Understand the difference between plants and animals

* Understand the water cycle
* Identify different types of rocks
* Identify phases of the moon
* Identify planets in the solar system
* Define the three major states of matter

* Classify changes as physical or chemical
* Understand a force is something that causes a change in motion or shape
* Recognize that magnetism and gravity are forces

HEALTH AND SAFETY

* Recognize the importance of fitness
* Identify healthy foods needed for a balanced diet

* Identify the function of these body systems: skeletal, respiratory, muscular, and circulatory
* Identify good dental health actions
* Understand how to control germs
* Identify careers in the health profession
* Be aware of harmful health practices, including drug and alcohol abuse
* Understand and respect the power of electricity
* Know safety rules regarding bike and pedestrian travel
* Know emergency procedures, such as calling 911
* Know and practice firesafety procedures
* Follow safety rules when playing
* Know how to handle being approached by a stranger
* Know what to do if someone touches them in an inappropriate way
* Know home safety rules, such as letting parents/guardians know where they are at all times

Living and Non-Living

Learning about the world around them is an important part of what third graders study in science classes. You can help your child by providing home experiences to support the school objectives.

Take a walk with your child around the house and outdoors. Locate an example of each of the characteristics below to demonstrate the difference between living and non-living.

Characteristic
* Living things grow, change, and repair themselves

Activities
* find a puppy and a dog
* look at a tiny plant and a large one
* find a tree where a branch broke off
* place a dry lima bean inside a plastic bag with a damp paper towel and watch it germinate

Characteristic
* Living things are made of cells

Activities
* scrape the inside of your cheek with a clean swab, rub the swab on a slide, and look at it under a microscope or very strong magnifying glass
* look at pictures of cells in an encyclopedia or science textbook

Characteristic
* Living things need energy

Activities
* discuss why we eat food
* talk about how plants get energy from the sun

Characteristic
* Living things respond to their environment

Activity
* set a plant in front of a bright window, watch it bend and grow toward the sunlight over a period of time

Characteristic
* Living things reproduce and create new life

Activities
* observe new plant sprouts
* look for baby animals in books, your neighborhood, or at the zoo
* talk about humans and their babies

Picture Fun—Encourage your child to find pictures or draw pictures of living and non-living things. Mark "L" on the living items in the picture and "N" on the non-living items.

A Terrific Terrarium—Create a terrarium in a large glass jar or aquarium. Put a layer of gravel in the bottom, next a layer of sand, and then a layer of potting soil. Add one or two small plants and some rocks. Talk about the difference between living and non-living. Introduce an earthworm or two and observe. Keep the terrarium covered unless condensation appears, then uncover it for a short time.

Brain Teaser: Gather a few non-living objects such as a pencil, a rock, and a hammer. Ask your child, "Were any parts of these items ever living?" (Remind your child that wood comes from trees!)

22 • BV15033 Home and School Success: Third Grade • Brighter Vision Publications

ROCKS AND SOIL

The best way to help your child learn about rocks and soil is to visit a variety of locations and dig around.

* At the park or near a lake, find a safe, little-traveled roadway or driveway filled with rocks. Work together to collect a variety of rocks and then classify them by color, size, shape, texture, or type.

* Read *Everybody Needs a Rock* by Byrd Baylor (Scribner, 1974). Discuss it with your child to increase awareness of the importance of our land and soil as a natural resource.

* Give your child two rocks that seem porous or crumbly. Holding the rocks above a dark piece of paper, let your child rub the two rocks together. By using a magnifying glass, your child will soon see that the sand on the paper is actually tiny rocks. This project demonstrates that soil is actually made of rocks being weathered and worn. Wind, water, and friction (such as your child has just created), cause that erosion of rock into soil.
Point out that some rocks are very soft, like chalk, and wear down quickly. Others are very hard, like granite or marble, and erode very slowly over thousands of years.

* Visit an agricultural office or nursery. They may have soil samples you can observe. Notice the color and texture differences.

* Place about 1 cup of soil in a quart jar of water. Put the lid on tight and shake it hard. Let it sit overnight without being moved. Notice the layers that have settled. The bottom layer will be sand and gravel, the middle layers will be silt and clay, and the top layer will be loam and humus. This lets your child see the types of soil you have in your area.

* Soil takes thousands of years to form so humans must use the land wisely. Watch for examples of ways people are using the land carefully such as terracing the land or planting windbreaks. Let your child fill a shallow plastic box or tray with sand or soil and add plastic trees, houses, and figures from the toy box. Stand back about 3 feet and aim a hair dryer at the box. Your child will quickly see the loss of soil that comes from wind. Tilt the box and repeat the experiment using a garden hose first with little water pressure and then with more pressure. Let your child try to replace the figures in a different way to prevent soil erosion.

MATTER REALLY MATTERS!

In many schools, third graders begin to explore the states of matter: liquids, solids, and gases. The more experiences you can provide to help your child discover the properties of these three states, the more quickly your child will connect with information provided in the classroom.

Characteristics of a solid:

* comes in different shapes and doesn't change shape easily
* can usually be seen
* is constructed of particles called molecules that are packed tightly together and do not move or move very slowly

Examples: ice, bricks, your hand

Characteristics of a liquid:

* can be poured and changes shape easily
* can usually be seen
* is constructed of particles called molecules that move and are not packed so tightly together as in a solid

Examples: milk, water, oil

Characteristics of a gas:

* can not always be seen but takes up space
* changes shape very easily
* is constructed of particles called molecules that are far apart and moving very quickly

Examples: air, helium, water vapor

The simplest way to demonstrate all three is to place an ice cube in a dish. While it is frozen, it is a solid. When it melts, it is a liquid. When it evaporates, it is a gas. Ask your child, "What causes the solid to become a liquid? What causes the liquid to become a gas?" Be sure to point out that heat created both changes.

WHAT MATTER IS IT?

Help your child identify the different states of matter. Select three containers you cannot see through. (Film canisters or yogurt cups with lids work well.) While your child is not watching, place rocks in one container, fill another ⅔ full of water, and leave the third "empty."

Using three small cards, have your child write *Solid* on one, *Liquid* on another, and *Gas* on the third. Allow your child to shake, listen, and examine the containers without removing the lids. After making a decision, have your child place the container on the card that names the matter inside. Ask your child to explain his or her reasoning. Refer to the descriptions on this page as a review if necessary. Now open the lids and congratulate your child's ability to discover information.

Make it harder! While your child is not watching, replace the rocks with cotton balls. Leave the other containers the same but move them around. (This is why it is important that all three containers are exactly alike.) Now let your child try to determine the three states of matter. Discuss your child's reasoning. Then let your child find examples and test you!

Social Studies Skills Third Graders Need

GEOGRAPHY, COMMUNITY, AND HERITAGE

* Locate their city, state, and country on a map
* Locate the United States on a globe
* Identify directions (N, S, E, and W) on a map
* Use a compass rose
* Interpret map symbols
* Begin to understand scale
* Create a map of a familiar area
* Identify the continents
* Know that about three-fourths of the earth is covered by water
* Explain geographical terms like river, lake, ocean, coast, island, mountain, forest, desert, and plain
* Understand that warmer climates are found near the equator and cooler climates occur near the poles
* Describe a community

* Describe the need for shelter, food, and clothing for all people
* Identify workers in a community
* Describe differences between rural and urban neighborhoods
* Identify different modes of transportation and the purpose of each
* Be aware of current events that involve their community
* Identify personal cultural heritage
* Express knowledge and interest in a variety of cultural holidays
* Value the diversity and recognize the commonality of ethnic groups and cultures within our country
* Recognize the purpose of national holidays
* Tell the importance of July 4
* Identify the contributions of famous Americans, such as George Washington, Abraham Lincoln, Susan B. Anthony, and Martin Luther King, Jr.

GOVERNMENT, ECOLOGY, AND GRAPHS

* Explain the reason for laws
* Discuss the fact that government leaders in the U.S. are elected
* Name a local leader
* Name the current U.S. president
* Know there are 50 states in the U.S.
* Know their own city, state, and state capital
* Explain the importance of conserving our natural resources

* Explain the meaning of "Reduce, Reuse, and Recycle"
* Interpret bar graphs
* Explain how a graph helps us understand information
* Begin to comprehend a circle graph

BV15033 Home and School Success: Third Grade • Brighter Vision Publications • 25

MAP SKILLS

Third graders are expected to begin to master some basic map skills that were introduced in earlier grades. Skills like interpreting symbols, understanding a legend, understanding scale, and using directions to locate places are critical to success in the social studies areas. You can help your child by using these skills in familiar and important settings.

Bedroom Map—Start by helping your child construct a flat map of his or her room. You may be planning to lay new carpet or rearrange the furniture. If so, get your child involved in the measuring and transferring of that information to paper.

Explain that this map is made as though you are sitting on the ceiling and looking down at the room. Encourage your child to design symbols that would indicate toy boxes, shelves, windows, doors, bed, chair, desk, or dresser. Using graph paper may make it easier for your child to draw items.

Street Map—Help your child design a simple map to show the way to school. Emphasize these items that help prevent the map user from getting lost: 1) a compass rose to indicate directions, and 2) clearly labeled streets. If possible, use the map and actually follow it. See if you and your child end up at school. Have your child make any necessary corrections and try it again!

Family Map—Have your child draw a rough map of your coummunity, state, or country, labeling where you and some of your favorite relatives live.

Direction Directions—Discuss with your child which way is north, south, east, and west in your house or yard. Play a "Simon Says" game using directions. Remind players to do only what "Simon Says" to do. Sample directives:

Simon says, "Walk 3 steps north."

Simon says, "Skip 4 steps east."

Simon says, "Walk 1 step south."

Simon says, "Walk 2 steps west."

In the beginning, you may need to write the direction words on index cards and actually lay them on the floor or grass in the matching locations. With enough practice, your child will know the correct way to move. If there are landforms or landmarks in your community that will help with directions, make sure to teach them. Examples: The mountains are west of town. The coast is south of here. The capital building is east of our neighborhood.

Hint: Help your child remember the clockwise order of the directions with this saying, "Never Eat Sour Watermelon!" (North, East, South, West)

COMMUNITY

Living and working with others in a community is a lifetime skill your third grader will need to master. It involves appreciating and respecting the feelings, heritage, and careers of other people, as well as expressing pride in the heritage and career of his or her own family. You can help your child learn to live and work in a community by providing experiences with community life.

Ant Farm—Set up an ant farm so that your child can observe the way ants create a community. Select a book from the public library or use the encyclopedia to describe the variety of jobs and chores that various ants assume. Explain how worker ants build the tunnels, nurse ants care for the young, the queen ant lays the eggs, and soldier ants guard the hill. As you discover how ants function in a community, build upon that information to help explain the larger communities that will be a part of your child's future. Have your child compare how ant and human communities are alike and how they are different.

Links in the Chain—A community needs all kinds of workers to meet the needs of its members and prosper. Brainstorm with your child a list of community workers—teachers, musicians, garbage collectors, doctors, park managers, and so on. Cut strips of paper. On each strip, have your child write the title of a community worker and draw pictures to match. Glue the strip ends together to make links and the links together to make a chain.

Which Community?—To illustrate the various levels of community of which your child is a member, make a list starting with family, neighborhood, city, county, state, country, planet, and galaxy. There are many other communities your third grader belongs to, such as his or her class at school, your place of worship, the Scout Group or 4-H Club, or the neighborhood soccer team.

> A community is a group of people (or sometimes animals) that live and work together to help all members of the community.

When the list is complete, draw a small circle in the middle of a huge piece of paper. (Newsprint is inexpensive and works great for this project.) In the center of the circle, have your child write his or her name. Then direct your child to draw another circle around that for the names of family members. Repeat the procedure and have your child fill in the next circle with the names of classmates. Continue out as far as your child has room, filling in circles with names of neighbors, local citizens, and so on.

CITIZENSHIP

The goal of good citizenship training is to create involved and knowledgeable leaders and citizenry for our future. You can help your child develop those skills by serving as a role model of an active and respectful citizen.

* Take your child to City Hall or the County Courthouse. Sign up for a tour if one is offered. If possible, have your child meet some of the community's leaders there.

* Create a family compact of rules and laws. Get everyone involved and accept ideas from everyone. Write them on a poster and display them where family members can view them daily. These rules will differ for each family.

* Express the things that are important to you as a family. Make rules for things that have not worked well in the past. Keep the rules short and easy to understand. Meet occasionally to review the rules and make changes. You can even hold an election to choose the "mayor" or the "secretary" for your family. Parents don't always have to be the leaders.

* Take your child with you when you vote. Discuss the issues and candidates beforehand. Explain your beliefs and encourage your child to share his or her opinions.

* Visit with your child about your volunteer activities in your community. Explain that everyone has the responsibility to participate in order for the community to thrive.

* Find a way that your child can get involved in volunteer activities within your community. Perhaps your child could become involved in a service project through a scout troop, school group, or community club. Charity organizations often need volunteers. Or contact your city hall, local chamber of commerce, or place of worship for ideas.

The members of this family promise to
. . . respect each other's ideas
. . . share time and talents
. . . be responsible for chores
. . . be considerate of each other
. . . be ready on time
. . . help one another

Help your child select a service activity that centers around his or her interests. For example, if your child loves animals, perhaps the local Humane Society could use a helper for cleaning and feeding the animals there. If your child likes gardening or planting, the park service in your city or a local senior citizens' home may appreciate help weeding and nurturing the flower plots. Explore the possibilities!

Art Skills Third Graders Need

Third graders enjoy art experiences and with their increased fine motor skills, they are ready for more involved processes. They also are excited about the results they produce.

At this age, they are becoming more aware of the world around them and are expanding their horizons to include appreciation of fine arts, diversity of cultural arts, feeling tones that art exhibits, and knowledge of the masters.

* Develop an awareness of art in nature
* Explore two-dimensional processes like drawing, painting, collage, mosaic, printmaking, and rubbings
* Examine the elements of design
* Incorporate different types of line in an original art work
* Understand the concept of space
* Use color hues and shades to create a variety of effects
* Experiment with textures
* Explore three-dimensional processes like clay sculpture and paper sculpture
* Experience weaving and stitchery
* Appreciate the individuality of art creations
* Demonstrate an increased sensitivity to what is art
* Explore emotions created by art
* Become aware of the work of some of the master artists
* Understand the difference between an original piece of art work and a reproduction

ARTISTIC ADVENTURES

Art expression is a spontaneous adventure that can occur almost anytime. Perhaps your child has just seen a beautiful butterfly and would like to create a similar pattern. Perhaps you and your child have just shared a wonderful story that inspired a picture. Whatever the occasion, be ready! Collect these things and keep them in an Art Box for those special times:

* Drawing paper of all sizes, colors, and types; odds 'n' ends; envelopes—lined and plain (Newspaper publishers often offer roll ends of newsprint at a very low cost.)
* All types of writing instruments—markers, crayons, pencils, chalk
* Clay or homemade dough (Mix 1 cup flour, ½ cup salt, 1 tablespoon alum, 1 tablespoon salad oil, 1 cup boiling water, and 1 teaspoon food coloring. Store in airtight container. Do *not* refrigerate.)
* Scissors—plain and fancy (The children's departments of many discount stores now carry inexpensive scissors that cut fancy shapes and are great fun to use.)
* Paint—water colors, tempera, or finger paint
* Paint tools—brushes, cotton swabs, feathers, sponges, string
* Boutique items—old jewelry, sequins, ribbons and trims, boxes, magazines
* Glue—school glue, craft glue, glue sticks (Glitter glue is fun, too!)

CRAYON CREATIONS

Melted Crayon Design—(BE SURE AN ADULT IS PRESENT AT ALL TIMES!) Light a used candle. Set it on an old cloth or newspaper. Peel the paper off some old crayons. Do *not* use short pieces. Hold the crayon in the flame until it starts to drip and then let the melted wax drip on the paper to make a design. Small projects are better done this way as it is a slow process.

Crayon Resist—Have your child create a simple design or picture on white paper. Direct your child to color over the design with dark, heavy crayon strokes. When the picture is complete, paint over it using a very light tempera or water color. This is a great technique for an ocean creation. Color bright tropical fish and wash over it with a light blue paint. Place plastic wrap over the front, frame it in black and you have an instant aquarium that never needs cleaning.

Sandpaper Surprises—Cover the table with newspaper. Give your child a square of rough grade sandpaper and have them color a design or picture right on it. Do not use words as they will transfer backwards.

Turn the sandpaper face down on a piece of plain paper and cover it with a layer of newspaper. Iron over the top. The iron has to be hot enough to melt the crayons. (AN ADULT SHOULD DO OR CAREFULLY SUPERVISE THIS PROCESS.) After it is cool enough to touch, carefully lift the corner and peel the paper back. The picture should have transferred to the paper.

PAINTING PROJECTS

Cotton Swab Painting—Paint a picture with tempera and cotton swabs. Dip the end of the swab in the paint and place a dot on the paper. Many dots, close together, begin to create the look of point painting used by some master artists, such as Georges Seurat. Continue dots of various colors until your creation is complete.

For variety use a cotton swab dipped in chlorine bleach (ADULT SUPERVISION REQUIRED) and make dots on a piece of very dark blue or black paper. It will bleach the color out so be sure you are working on a pad of newspaper. This makes wonderful snow or nighttime sky designs.

Feather Painting—This technique will give you a whimsical, light look. It is a great way to get the clouds in a bright summer picture. Dip the feather lightly into white paint and stroke lightly across the skyline on blue paper or a blue painted background.

Blow Art—Dribble thin tempera across a piece of paper. Get very close to the paint and blow through a straw to move the paint around and create the look you want.

Music Skills Third Graders Need

Music is an important part of the curriculum and our everyday lives. Third graders love singing, tapping, echoing, clapping, moving, listening, plucking, and playing.

TEMPO, DYNAMICS, DURATION, AND TONE

* Identify the speed of the beat: slow, fast, getting slower, getting faster
* Use tempo to express different styles
* Distinguish between soft, very soft, loud, and very loud tones
* Associate those with music terms: piano (p), pianissimo (pp), forte (f), fortissimo (ff)
* Sing or play an instrument to demonstrate these terms
* Demonstrate an understanding of meter, rhythm, and length of notes
* Identify and respond to musical symbols
* Practice singing or playing a scale up and down

FORM AND STYLE

* Identify, reproduce, and create verse and refrain patterns
* Recognize and sing or move to a variety of musical styles from various cultures
* Recognize and sing rounds

MUSIC APPRECIATION

* Respond to and enjoy a variety of music
* Identify instruments and their "families"
* Become aware of the works of great composers and musicians
* Recognize the qualities of good singing
* Participate in musical activities

MAKE MUSICAL MAGIC WITH YOUR CHILD!

Draw What You Hear—Respond to music with your child. Share a giant piece of paper and some crayons. As you both listen to some interesting music, just let the crayons flow down the paper. When the song is completed, talk about what you felt when you made certain designs on the picture.

For a variation on this activity, decide before you listen, how to respond to a certain tempo or pitch. Perhaps you want to use dots when the tempo is fast and lines when the music slows. Perhaps you want to use circles when the pitch is low and triangles when the pitch is high. When the song is finished, take a look at your artistic response to that music.

Let's Move—You can also respond with your child through movement. Move like an elephant when the music is slow or like a bee when it is fast. Put your hands up when the pitch is high and down when it is low. Scarves, strips of cloth, or crepe paper streamers can add a new dimension to responding to music. Be sure you give yourselves plenty of room for this activity.

Rewrite It—Make up new words to old tunes. For example, instead of "Mary Had a Little Lamb" perhaps "Mary Had a Loaf of Bread!" Some of the lyrics will get silly and giggles will result from this fun activity. This is a great game to play while riding in the car. It is also good to connect the lyrics to a topic your child is studying at school.

Echo Sing—Echo singing results when one partner sings a line and the other sings it back. You don't have to be a great singer to enjoy this with your child. Just make your voice use different pitches, rhythms, and tempos to make your child aware of the variety.

Whose Voice?—Use different voices. First sing an old familiar song like "Here We Go 'Round the Mulberry Bush" in your regular voice. Next sing it in a very deep voice like a dinosaur might have sung it. Then try it the way a tiny fairy might sing it using a high pitched voice. Have fun by wiggling your index finger quickly between your lips as you sing like a goldfish underwater!

Physical Education Skills Third Graders Need

Physical fitness is one key to a healthy, balanced life. Physical education gives children a chance to learn about their bodies through sports and games. Physical education focuses on strength, balance, flexibility, and endurance. Third graders usually learn the skills required to play popular sports, but most games are simplified, less competitive versions. The other key component of physical education is learning to play and work together.

PRESIDENT'S COUNCIL ON PHYSICAL FITNESS

These are the activities established by the President's Council to demonstrate fitness. The requirements vary by age and sex.

* Curl ups
* Shuttle run
* Sit and reach
* One mile run/walk
* Pull-ups
* Flexed-arm hang

FAMILY FITNESS FUN

Family fitness fun should just be a part of your everyday lives. Modeling good wellness routines important to you and adding fitness in a fun way is the perfect addition to that philosophy.

* Whenever possible, walk or ride bikes instead of driving to school, the library, the store, or a park.
* Get the whole family involved in a team sport like softball or basketball.
* If your child has a special sports interest try to become actively involved or at least become knowledgeable of the rules. Your child will feel supported and valued because of your interest.
* Try to spend at least half an hour outside with your child each day. Perhaps you can play catch, fly a kite, or just go for a walk.
* Involve your child as much as you can in sports you enjoy. Create awareness in your child for lifetime leisure time activities.

FITNESS AND ATTITUDE

* Cross the horizontal ladder
* Jog for five minutes
* Jump rope for endurance
* Bounce, throw, and catch a ball
* Perform warm-up exercises
* Perform simple rhythmic activities
* Accept responsibilities as a team player
* Demonstrate good sportsmanship
* Participate safely
* Give top effort
* Play fair
* Take care of equipment
* Respect other students and teachers
* Follow directions

PHYSICAL FITNESS FUN!

Jump the Ball!—You will need a ball attached to a nine-foot-long rope. (A punch ball which you can buy at discount stores works great.) One person stands in the middle and twirls the ball around in a circle. Be sure the ball just skims the top of the ground or floor. The other person stands about nine feet away. As the ball comes around, the outside person attempts to jump over the ball without being touched. If the ball is touched at all, the two trade places. The spinner can increase or decrease the speed of the ball to trick the jumper.

Stop the Ball!—This is a variation of the above game. One person sits down on the perimeter of the circle while the other person spins the ball. The object is to flick your feet out and stop the ball as it passes by.

Balloon Walk—This game is more fun and more challenging with a lot of players. For best results, play on a hard surface area. Tie a balloon with a cord or strong ribbon to the ankle of every player. The object is to break the balloon on the other players' legs without allowing your own balloon to be broken!

Keep it up!—Blow up an extra large balloon. Toss it up in the air and bounce it back and forth, trying to keep it from touching the ground. A player who allows it to touch the ground gets a penalty letter. The letters should spell out " b-a-l-l-o-o-n". If you are the first to spell the whole word, the other player wins. You can play this game with a group. Each player is eliminated as they spell "balloon." The last player left in the game is the winner.

Indoor Hoops—Create safe balls out of wadded up newspaper wrapped with masking tape. Each player should have four of them. Write the players' initials on all of their balls. Set an empty wastebasket a certain distance away depending upon your child's ability to throw and mastery of eye-hand coordination. At a signal, both players start throwing the balls toward the wastebasket. Only one throw per ball. When all the balls have been tossed, add up the score. You get one point for each ball that landed inside the wastebasket. Each round you play, move back from the wastebasket by one foot. You can keep score, or you can graph the number player A got in at six feet, at seven feet, and so on. Have players keep their own graph going as far as the game goes to find their personal best range. The latter method of scoring eliminates competition between players and focuses on improving your own personal skills.

34 • BV15033 Home and School Success: Third Grade • Brighter Vision Publications

Social Skills Third Graders Need

Although academics are the main thrust of your child's education, he or she cannot succeed at school without some basic social skills. This next section will address several key areas, including respect, responsibility, classroom interactions, problems with peers, manners, and safety issues.

RESPECT FOR OTHERS

Listen—Discuss with your child the importance and benefits of listening to others and their opinions. You can explain that everyone has differences of opinions and everyone has the right to express those opinions. Even if you don't agree with others' ideas, you still need to respectfully listen, and then you can have the opportunity to express your point of view. Demonstrate your respect for your child by listening to his or her opinions. This provides an excellent model through which your child can see how important it is to respect other people.

> The Golden Rule—"Treat others as you would like them to treat you" is the foundation of working, playing, and getting along with others. Your home is the place your child should first learn and practice the Golden Rule, then he or she will be able to apply it to peer, school, and community situations.

Cultural Diversity—Third graders are ready to appreciate the diversity of people and are alert to likenesses and differences. Encourage your child to ask questions and explore ethnic diversity in your community. Invite guests from other cultures or lands to share their customs if you have the opportunity. Cook foreign dishes on occasion or dine at ethnic restaurants and bazaars to sample foods of different cultures. Speak positively of the contributions of people from many backgrounds.

RESPECT FOR ONESELF

Third graders are already aware of the times when they do their best work. They are proud of those efforts and excited to share their feelings with adults. The attention you are paying through daily interactions will allow your child to feel safe, secure, and worthy. A child with a sense of self-worth will demonstrate it by standing up for himself or herself and for the ideals parents have nurtured. This same child will be less likely to be coaxed or lured into dangerous or destructive situations. He or she has the confidence to express and pursue goals, to withstand peer pressures better, and to explore new horizons. Encourage your child to be his or her own best friend!

We're Proud of You—Recognize your child's strengths and "broadcast" those abilities. You don't need to report it on the national news, but display it proudly where your child can see it every day. Set up a bulletin board or an area on the refrigerator for each of your children. Exhibit good schoolwork, proud photos, notes of love and praise, and special awards. Be creative and proud!

RESPECT FOR AUTHORITY

People—The teachers, principal, secretaries, and other support staff who work at your child's school are there because they care about children. Teach your child that those people are responsible for the safety and success of the school and they can't do their jobs without respect from all members of the school community. Discuss examples of showing respect for authority, such as speaking in a considerate manner and following directions.

School Rules

* Use an appropriate voice.
* Give your best effort.
* Use your time wisely.
* Ask questions if you don't understand.
* Respect the thoughts and feelings of others.
* Be responsible and dependable.
* Participate in all activities.
* Work and play safely.
* Take care of school property.

Rules

Get a copy of your child's school handbook and ask the teacher for a list of rules that are established for the classroom. Some typical ones are noted in the gray box on the left.

Discuss the rules with your child. Be sure he or she understands not only the rule, but the reason for the rule.

If any of the school's rules conflict with your household rules, discuss them with your child. Help your child understand the importance of following the rules for whatever community he or she is visiting—school, a friend's home, another country. If there is a school rule that strongly contradicts your personal or religious beliefs, speak with your child's teacher. Many times an alternative can be agreed to that achieves the same goal and respects the rights of all.

RESPECT FOR PROPERTY

* Discuss the many ways we care for property, such as putting things back where they belong, asking before borrowing, using equipment properly, or picking up litter on the playground.
* As you drive past an example of vandalism or graffiti, point it out to your child. Explain the destructiveness of such acts. Emphasize the lack of respect they demonstrate. Help your child empathize with the people who have to clean up, fix, or replace the damaged property. Follow up with information regarding the punishments for such behavior. Remind your child that all choices have consequences.

> Children need to take care of their own property and that of the school. They also need to respect the things that belong to their classmates.

36 • BVI5033 Home and School Success: Third Grade • Brighter Vision Publications

RESPONSIBILITY

Your child needs to be independent in applying learning strategies and able to be relied upon by you to complete a task. A child who is dependent on the parent for decision making and goal setting is handicapped for life.

* The most basic way to teach your child responsibility is through chores. Hold a family meeting and together make a list of the things that need to get done in order for the family to live in a clean, safe, and healthy home. Let family members first sign up for daily and weekly chores they want to do. Then see what's left! Encourage everyone to be involved in a fair solution for dividing and assigning the remaining chores. Set guidelines for when chores need to be finished. Then let children take responsibility for doing them or losing the privilege of playing or participating in extra-curricular activities.

* Arrange situations where your child can make important choices. It could be as simple as, "We need one dozen doughnuts. Please choose an assortment for us." Of course, when you allow your child to make choices you must accept that decision without redirection, so choose the situation carefully.

* Occasionally a child who is allowed to make choices and decisions that are important will assume that family or parent decisions are now under his or her control. You can manage this situation by explaining that some choices belong to third graders and some choices belong to adults.

* Assist your child in becoming responsible by establishing a location by the door or on a special shelf where lunch money, library books, permission slips, and homework should always be placed. This spot should be easily accessible to your child. Reinforce the use of this collection spot until it becomes a habit for your child. Point out how much smoother the morning goes when everything that is needed for the day is in one location.

wash dishes
bathe dog
water plants

Your child will be responsible for his or her actions or assignments only if you do not take the responsibility for those tasks yourself.

* When your child makes a choice to be involved in an activity, such as a class play, piano lessons, or soccer team, it is important to stress the commitment of that decision. Responsible adults learned in their early years that once you have dedicated your efforts, completing the task or event is vital. Stress the fact that others are depending on each individual in order for the event to be successful.

* All of us fail to be reliable or dependable at some time when we forget or avoid a task. Be understanding. Teach your child that if an effort to be reliable fails, the best policy is to be honest and not to blame others for your failure. If your child forgets lunch money, he or she should tell the teacher. If your child ran out of time to finish the homework, he or she should write the note explaining why. If your child forgot to walk the dog, the child should be honest and tell the adult involved.

CLASSROOM INTERACTIONS

A Wide Range of Students—Children come in all shapes, sizes, and abilities and all have their own strengths and weaknesses. Your child needs to know how to interact with children who may be quicker or slower, rude or considerate, shy or bossy, physically challenged or athletic, or many other combinations.

Help your child be aware of the uniqueness of each classmate and how important each one is to the class. Encourage your child to write a kind note to a classmate or to pass on compliments periodically. Everyone likes to be appreciated!

Act out "pretend" situations that might occur in the classroom. This will help your child be prepared to meet those challenging times. For example, if another child is coaxing your child to refuse to play with a handicapped classmate, you could be your child and demonstrate exactly what you would say and do to stand up for the classmate who is being excluded. Your child could "play" the part of the "ring-leader" and try to get you to cooperate in the conspiracy. Later your child could "play" the part of the handicapped friend so that the feelings of being ignored could be explored. Scenarios like this could come right from after-school conversations that clue you in on what is worrying your child.

Group members
- listen
- give ideas
- take turns
- work hard even if their idea wasn't chosen

Cooperative Groups—Being able to work with a partner, a small group, or the entire class, is an important part of your child's learning. Ask your child which activities he or she likes to do alone and which with a group. Talk about reasons your child likes or dislikes solitary or group activities.

If your child has trouble working in groups, you can help your child by comparing learning groups to your family. Everyone has certain jobs to do so that all the work gets done. Then everyone benefits by getting to do fun things together. Encourage your child to be a team player. Make a list of what things individuals need to do in order for the group to succeed. Have your child identify areas where he or she and other group members need to improve.

Asking for Help

If your child indicates confusion about assignments, find out if he or she asks the teacher for help when needed. Try to determine why your child doesn't understand something. Write a note or call the teacher if your child indicates further lack of understanding or a fear of asking for help.

PROBLEM SOLVING

Every journey through life includes a few bumps. And some children and adults will experience several! You can help your child by leading him or her through a process to try whenever a problem arises.

Use the picture below to "walk" your child through the "steps" of problem solving. It might be helpful to copy this chart and actually write out some of the steps with your child. This process should be completed using several different types of problems, including a behavioral concern, a science experiment, or a mathematical problem. The benefit for your child will come in repeating the process. It allows him or her to approach a problem with a logical thought process instead of reacting without thinking things through.

The best way to demonstrate how well this works is for you to apply it to a simple problem you are trying to solve at home. Talk it through out loud with your child and explain each level of the procedure as you go. Celebrate the results when it is completed, or point out that it may be necessary to repeat some steps to solve the problem.

Fairness is an important concern, especially for children. If your child is considering ideas for solving a behavioral or social problem, ask him or her to evaluate whether each solution is a "fair" one.

1. Say the problem out loud.
2. Explore some ideas.
3. Think about what might happen with each idea.
4. Choose an idea.
5. Do it!
6. Rethink it. (Go back two steps if needed.)
7. Celebrate the solution!

Home and School Cooperation

COMMUNICATING WITH YOUR CHILD'S TEACHER

Because time is so limited in everyone's busy schedule, communication is often short and single-focused. Everyone experiences the same time restraints and the frustration it causes. For that reason, when you need to contact your child's teacher, be specific and considerate of the school schedule.

* Contact the teacher with positive comments as well as concerns.

* Keep the conversation on topic. Discuss only the essentials.

* Try to share concerns and suggestions as efficiently as possible.

* Offer to help solve a problem or concern. Make suggestions carefully so as not to indicate concern about the teacher's ability to handle it.

* Keep conversations with the teacher confidential especially if other students are involved.

* If you have a request, make it in writing by sending a note with your child.

* Keep a sense of humor about classroom situations and share it with the teacher.

* Respond to class projects by sending a note or making a phone call to express your pride at your child's work.

* If you offer to help in the classroom, be prompt.

* Offer curriculum support with materials or resource people.

COMMUNICATING WITH YOUR CHILD'S SCHOOL ADMINISTRATOR

* When you see or hear about something positive and exciting happening at the school, call the administrator or send a note.

* If you have a question about the reason for a school rule, contact the administrator with that question. Approach it with curiosity or concern, not animosity.

* If disagreements arise, explain your viewpoint calmly and have a reason for your opinion.

* Participate in parent groups by attending meetings and volunteering whenever possible.

* Attend board meetings to become better informed about school policy.

TOP TEN WAYS FOR COMMUNICATING WITH YOUR CHILD

1 Focus on the relationship with your child. Demonstrate your love every day! A child who experiences love flourishes in all aspects of life.

2 Listen to your child. Even though the topic may not interest you, pay attention.

3 Model patience and teach it. Then when you are busy and ask your child to be patient and wait, he or she will believe you. When you ask for patience, you will need to insist on it and not give in or become irritated.

4 Be ready to admit that you are not perfect! Recognize that you will make mistakes and talk to your child about it. Show him or her that mistakes or failures are a part of the learning process. Don't hesitate to admit you don't know something. Just be ready to find out.

5 Encourage independence. Over-protection handicaps children in every avenue of life. You certainly want your child to have roots, but you must also be ready to offer wings to fly, explore, and make his or her own mistakes.

6 Maintain a sense of humor. Accidents will happen. Plans will fall apart. Try to laugh at yourself and at the quirks in everyday life.

7 Set guidelines and stick to them. Consistency is very important as it provides children with stability in their lives. Children need and want lines of behavior drawn and they need to know that those don't change with the whims of the day. Discipline should be directed at the act, not the child.

8 Stay focused on the long-term goal of raising a happy, healthy child who will contribute in a positive way to society. Many pitfalls will occur along the way. Try not to worry about the minor events.

9 Spend time with your child. Include your child in your activities and get involved in the things that interest him or her. The quantity of time is important, but it's the quality of that time that reaps great rewards.

10 Most important of all, practice what you preach. If you want your child to respect and uphold your examples and decisions, then follow the same rules of respect and responsibility that you teach.

CREATING COOPERATIVE CONFERENCES

Conferences come in all shapes and sizes! Some may be formally planned and scheduled. Others may be impromptu and informal. Some may include several people who work with the child. Some may include only the teacher and you. Others may include your child. You and the classroom teacher generally make the decisions as to how a conference is to be organized. Once that is established, the important goal is to make that conference productive for your child's learning process.

The teacher will come with documentation and observations of how your child functions in the classroom. It is like the teacher has a photograph in his or her mind of your child as a classroom learner.

You should also come with ideas and information about how your child functions at home. It is like you have a photograph in your mind of how your child learns at home.

My child learns best by . . .

My child worries about . . .

My child likes . . .

My child does not like . . .

My child is confused about . . .

The object is to combine those two photographs into a picture that is more nearly what your child is truly like.

You and the teacher will share ideas each work with your child in each setting. You will share strengths, abilities, gifts, and areas that need improvement. The sharing that occurs at a conference of any type is what will create a better situation for your child.

Here are some conference tips:

✱ **If you don't understand something the teacher said, ask for it to be repeated and explained.**

✱ **Be sure you stay focused on the topic of the conference which is your child, not your neighbor's child.**

✱ **Don't schedule a conference if you are angry. Get your emotions in check first and then approach in a rational way.**

✱ **Use phrases like "Can you tell me more about that situation?"**

✱ **Bring these notes with you:**

I had a question about _____

I am confused about _____

I really like _____

I wanted you to know that _____

VOLUNTEERING

There are many benefits to being an involved parent:

* Your child is proud of your help and knows you support the school and its educational activities
* You learn how the class operates and the expectations the teacher holds
* You meet the children your child interacts with
* You are more aware of classroom topics and schoolwide concerns
* The teacher knows you care and thinks of your child every time he or she sees you

Here are some ways your help would really HELP!

> Most teachers encourage parents to become involved at school. They will appreciate any assistance you can give whether it is a one-time special event or help on a regular basis.

At school, working with children:

* Listen to children read
* Do flashcard drills
* Help with creative writing
* Assist in the computer lab
* Give a book talk on a children's book you read
* Share a special talent or hobby
* Work with a small group for a short-term project—science fair, book discussion groups, etc.

At home:

* Type or do word processing
* Write notes or letters
* Translate forms
* Tape-record books for listening libraries
* Prepare snacks
* Plan holiday celebrations
* Recruit resource people

At school, working without children:

* Put up bulletin boards
* Maintain the classroom or school library
* Prepare materials for lessons
* File student work
* Cut out and laminate materials
* Assemble packets for the school
* Work a shift at special events—book fair, auction, carnival, garage sale, etc.

Volunteers Are Great!

Good with children
Ready on time
Enormously important
Appreciated by all
Truly make a difference!

HOMEWORK

Have you ever tried to bake a cake and discovered you had no flour? It requires a quick trip to the store. When you return, you find that the pan is dirty and has to be washed. Then you can't find a rubber scraper to clean the bowl. By the time you get the cake done, you are totally frustrated.

Your child will feel the same way if you expect him or her to complete homework without the right tools. Assemble the items listed in the box on the right. Then create a workspace where everything is organized and ready to use.

Above the workspace, which could be a desk or table top, hang a bulletin board or spare ceiling tiles. Your child can pin notes, a calendar, and a schedule up there for easy reference.

In this book you will find many notes or guides that would be good to display at your child's workspace:

* SEARCH cue card (page 6)
* SCOPE editing tips (page 11)
* spelling procedure (page 13)
* penmanship guides (pages 14–15)
* math problem-solving strategies (page 20)

Encourage your child to make a schedule each night. Have your child jot down what homework has been assigned and mark what needs to be done first. Some children like to do the hard tasks first, others like to get the easy ones done first. Let your child choose, and then check to see if the schedule plan is working.

Homework Supplies

* Variety of types of paper including plain, lined, and colored paper
* Scrap paper to be used for notes (Recycle the backs of used sheets, mail that came with nothing on the back, or mistakes from the computer printer.)
* Pens and pencils (Be sure the pens have ink and the pencils have points.)
* Pencil sharpener
* Erasers—either a large art one or ones on the ends of pencils
* Ruler—one with both metric and customary markings
* Scissors
* Crayons and markers
* Glue, paste, or rubber cement
* Dictionary
* Atlas or globe

Bookmarks

Rewards

YOU really hopped to it!

"Every bunny" is proud of you!

Here's the scoop...

Your work has been terrific!

You have many gifts! But the best gift of all... is YOU!

YOU are on the ROAD to SUCCESS!

CELEBRATE You should be very proud!

Backs of Bookmark Rewards